I know I can!
Make my Bed

ANTHEA DAVIDSON-JARRETT
Illustrated by
Aldana Penayo
Published by EDUCATE THE GLOBE,
London, UK, 2022.

ISBN: 978-1-913804-05-3

Copyright © 2022 Educate The Globe Limited. All rights reserved. No part of this book is to be reprinted, copied or stored in retrieval systems of any type, except by written permission from the author. Part of this book may, however, be used only in reference to support related documents or subjects.

Artwork featured: Buckley, Omar (2017)
Ast and Nebhet Praising Ra,
Ramomar NY, New York.

I know I can do it!

Please can I help?

I want to do it all by myself!

Please can I try?

Can you show me how?

I'm not too small,

I am ready right now!

It's Saturday and

I've just woken up.

Time to make my bed

before I walk my pup.

Mummy says that

I am big enough now

so she will take the time

to show me how.

First I have to clear my bed

and make sure that

all the toys go in the box.

Mummy gives me a hand.

Pillows on the table!

Duvet on my chair!

Who is watching in the corner?

It's Mocha! My big cuddly bear.

Now we spread the bed sheet

over my bed.

Wrap the corners of the mattress

at the bottom and the head.

Smooth out the sheet;

no creases or wrinkles!

It takes lots of practice

to do it without crinkles.

Mummy is a pro!

She does it very fast.

Lays the top sheet over

With a super duper blast!

The sides must be equal;

no dragging on the floor.

Mummy folds the corners

without a single flaw.

Now we lay the duvet;

the sides must be equal.

Mummy throws it up!

It flies and lands like an eagle.

Leave space for the pillows!

Fold the top sheet and duvet over.

Tuck the edges under the mattress..

we are the 'Bed Composers'!

Now for the part after

the pillow case stuffing...

Pat! Pat! Squeeze! Squeeze!

This is pillow fluffing!

Lay the pillows at the head;

I have two!

If you have a big bed

four or six will do!

Sit Mocha comfortably

back at the end.

Phew! That was like a workout;

I can't pretend!

Making my bed wasn't easy

but now I know how.

"Thank-you for your help mummy!

I'm off to walk my puppy now."